What the World Eats

MIDDAY MEAL

TOM AND JENNY WATSON

CHILDRENS PRESS INTERNATIONAL

What the World Eats

Breakfast
Midday Meal
Evening Meal

2.29.84 pub 8.45

Library of Congress Cataloging in Publication Data
Watson, Tom.
Midday meal.

(What the world eats)
Bibliography: p.
Includes index.
Summary: Describes the varying midday eating habits of
people in all parts of the world and the food they choose to
eat, whether as a light snack or in a full meal.
1. Luncheons—Juvenile literature. 2. Food habits—
Juvenile literature. 3. Cookery, International—Juvenile
literature. [1. Luncheons. 2. Food habits] I. Watson, Jenny.
II. Title. III. Series: Watson, Tom. What the world eats.
TX735.W37 1983 394.1'6 W33 82-19908
ISBN 0-516-01857-4

1983 American Edition published by
Childrens Press International

© Copyright 1982 Wayland Publishers Ltd, England

Phototypeset by Direct Image,
Hove, East Sussex
Printed in Italy by G. Canale & C.S.p.A., Turin
Bound in the U.S.A.

Contents

Left *This family is able to eat the midday meal or lunch together, but other families may be apart at work or school.*

Below *On a fine day we may enjoy a picnic outside.*

1 · What we eat

Do you look forward to your midday meal all morning? Perhaps it is your main meal of the day, or maybe it is more of a snack. What do you eat? Is it a full cooked meal with a dessert to follow, or sandwiches, or just a bag of potato chips? The type of midday meal, or lunch, we eat may depend on many things.

If you are at school, school lunches are available, but if you do not like those, you may bring your own packed lunch. Your parents may give you money to go out and buy something to eat —so then the choice is up to you. What sort of a meal do you eat —is it good for you? It is important for us all to have a well-balanced diet, which means eating different foods that are individually rich in the nutriments. Our bodies need different foods for good health. School lunch menus are carefully worked out to make sure that they provide balanced meals. A packed lunch can be just as nutritious if you take the trouble to plan what goes in it. But if you have money to spend on your midday meal, what do you buy? Chips, cookies or candy might be your favorites—but these will not provide you with a very nutritious meal.

Some people eat in cafeterias and restaurants and some eat at home. Cost, convenience, time, whether we prefer a big or a small meal—all these things affect what we eat in the middle of the day.

A cooked meal

What do you call your midday meal? It may be either 'lunch' or 'dinner,' depending upon where you come from. The size of your meal may vary, too—from a traditional three-course dinner to a smaller one of a main course followed by a piece of fruit. A full meal will perhaps begin with soup, followed by meat, potatoes and vegetables, ending with a sweet dessert of some kind. A smaller meal might consist of macaroni and cheese, pizza, hamburger and french fries, or a salad, followed by fresh fruit or maybe just a drink. Many of these dishes are popular for the evening meal, too.

Many people like to cook a bigger meal on a Sunday and make more of an occasion out of it. It may be the only day of the week that the family is able to sit down and eat together. A

Below *Toasted sandwiches make an appetizing snack meal.*

Right *Choosing what to eat is the customer's biggest problem in this cafeteria.*

traditional Sunday dinner has a meat dish accompanied by potatoes, vegetables, gravy, and maybe stuffing. This is followed by a dessert and coffee.

Your cooked meal could be more of a snack—think of hot dogs or a toasted sandwich.

Which type of meal do you prefer? Is it different from the one that you usually eat? We may eat a certain type of meal just out of habit, for convenience, because it is put in front of us, or because we cannot afford the type of meal that we would really like!

Packed lunches and school lunches

Left *An office worker eats lunch at her desk.*

Right *School lunches — how popular are they at your school?*

Packed lunches (also known as sack lunches or box lunches) are popular for midday meals because they are easier and cheaper than going out for lunch in a restaurant. People in all occupations—those who work in offices, on building sites, and factories—often take a lunch with them. All over the world children take a packed meal to school. Many do this because they do not like the school lunches!

Sandwiches filled with a variety of savory foods—cheese, ham, chicken, egg, corned beef, various salads—are usually the main part of a packed lunch. Packets of potato chips, peanuts, fruit, yogurt, perhaps something sweet like a piece of cake, a cookie, or candy bar may also be included.

It is important that your packed lunch should be a balanced meal, like all your other meals. It should contain some body-building *protein*, like a cheese or meat filling in the sandwiches; *carbohydrates* from bread, cookies, or cake to give energy and warmth; the *vitamins* and *minerals* essential to good health from fruit, milk, fruit juice, and salad vegetables; and *fats* for energy and warmth from butter or chocolate.

Since the Second World War, many children living in the United States have been offered a cooked school lunch. These are balanced meals made up of a main dish with a dessert to follow. School lunches are subsidized by the government, which means that the government pays part of the cost of the meal, but most parents must still pay the rest. What do you think about your school lunches? You could try doing a survey among your classmates.

In Australia, all children take a packed lunch as there is no school lunch service. Usually they eat their sandwiches outside in an open-fronted building called a weather shed, but when the weather is bad they eat in their classrooms.

In Great Britain, school lunches are subsidized, too. Like American children, many British students take sandwiches to school for lunch.

Take-out meals

Some people like take-out meals. Instant meals like these save you the time and trouble of preparing your own. There are take-out restaurants of many kinds in most towns and cities, but which sort have been around the longest? Hamburger and hotdog shops! There is probably one near where you live. Foreign take-out restaurants of all descriptions have increasingly appeared on our streets—Chinese for foods like chow mein, fried rice, and egg rolls; Italian for pizzas; Greek for kebabs.

You probably have a favorite among these. Take-out meals are certainly convenient, but do they have any disadvantages? Cost is one—you could prepare the same meal more cheaply at home. What about the nutritive value of these meals—do they contain the foods necessary for good health? Very greasy foods like some hamburgers and french fries contain rather more fat than is good for us, but the basic ingredients of meat and potatoes contain protein, carbohydrates, and vitamins and

Fish and chips—the first popular take-out meal in Great Britain.

Choosing a hamburger at a MacDonald's fast food take-out restaurant.

minerals—a fairly balanced meal. Try working out what nutriments other take-out meals supply us with.

Hamburgers and french fries are usually freshly cooked when we buy them, but some take-out foods may have been reheated several times. Cooking food again like this can destroy some of its nutritive value. You do not always know what you are getting, either. How much meat is actually in your hamburger? A large part of it may be made from cereal, which is not a protein food like meat.

Why we eat these things

Everybody enjoys eating—so trying out new foods that manufacturers have made can be fun. On television, in magazines, and on billboards, advertisements tempt us to buy these new foods.

How do advertisements persuade us to buy a product? We might think that the message that the manufacturer uses is a sensible one—perhaps the food contains extra vitamins and will 'do us good.' Our appetites might be aroused by the look of

This mouthwatering display advertises a cooked meat manufacturer's products.

MEALZ ON WHEELZ!

*Many ads for foods feature
the young consumers that
the product is aimed at.*

the food. We may be flattered and think we are more know-ledgeable and sophisticated if we buy a certain product. The ad might try to play on the things we may worry about—it may try to convince us that we will be more popular if we buy a certain brand of soft drinks, which would immediately bring new friends flocking round! It may try to persuade our mothers that they will be more popular with us if they give us a particular brand of food to eat. Or if a product is often advertised, we may think that a lot of people must like it—so perhaps we should, too.

So, we buy a certain product—then, because we like the taste of it, the way it is advertised and packaged—we keep on buying it. We have developed a 'brand loyalty.'

Try making a list of food advertisements, and see if you can work out which of your emotions the manufacturer is trying to appeal to.

Foreign and convenience foods

Today, many of our most popular meals are dishes which we may think of as our own, but which originally came from other countries. Did you know that spaghetti, lasagna, ravioli, and pizza all come from Italy? Pizzas, in particular, have become very popular and you can find pizzerias (pizza restaurants) in many towns. India has given us curry and chutney, China has introduced us to many of her dishes like fried rice, sweet and sour pork, and egg rolls. We eat moussaka from Greece, kebabs from the Middle East, chili con carne (a hot, spicy meat dish) from Mexico, and quiche lorraine (egg and bacon pie) from France. Can you think of any others?

Left *Many of us enjoy Chinese food—just think how many Chinese restaurants and take-outs you see.*

Above *Italian pizza has become so popular that we no longer really think of it as a 'foreign' dish.*

15

Convenience foods—why do we have them? Because many people lead busy lives, they want food that is easy to prepare and quick to cook, and yet is nutritious and interesting to eat. Food companies produce convenience foods to meet these demands, and also strive to invent completely new dishes, which attract people by their novelty just as much as by their usefulness. There are instant desserts to which you need add only milk or water. There are cans of soup, ravioli, spaghetti, beef stew, and chicken casserole. There are sauce mixes, quick-cooking rice, dried potato pieces, and ready-sliced bread. There are whole meals packed into a sectioned plastic bag, which you just pop into boiling water to heat, then cut open and serve. The list of foods is almost endless; perhaps you can add to those already mentioned.

Left *The ingredients for chop suey — but this meal came out of a box and took only fifteen minutes to make.*

Above *This complete chicken dinner only needs to be heated through in the oven.*

All these convenience foods, however, may not be as nourishing as freshly-prepared meals. Food which is cooked twice—which convenience foods are—may have some of its nutriments destroyed.

Have you ever looked at the list of ingredients which is printed on the can? You will see that most of these foods contain a bewildering assortment of additives. Manufacturers use these not only to preserve the food, but to change its appearance, taste, or texture as well. All additives have been tested and are presumed to be harmless in small quantities, but nobody knows the effects of eating them over a very long period of time.

Have you eaten any convenience foods today?

Where does our food come from?

Although we produce some of the food that we eat, we also buy food from other countries. This might be because our climate is not suitable for growing a certain food, or because another country can grow it more cheaply. We may be in the middle of winter, but a country on the other side of the world might be having its summer, and will be busy growing the vegetables or fruit that we want.

If you look at the labels on food in the shops, you will find that our food comes from many different parts of the world. There is cheese from The Netherlands, bacon from Denmark, ham from Poland, canned tomatoes from Italy, and canned fruit from Thailand. The U.S.A., Canada, and Australia sell grain for making bread and cereals to other countries. New Zealand, South America, and Australia export large quantities of meat.

Why not look at the food in the cupboard at home to see where it comes from. Make a list—you will be surprised at how many different countries' names you will collect.

Packing crates with oranges in a South African factory.

2 · What people in other countries eat

This map shows you the
countries that we are going
to look at in this chapter.

North

America

South

America

All around the world the midday meal is treated in different ways. In some countries the midday meal is not so important. People will only take a short break while they are at work or school and the shops and factories will stay open and running. Here the midday or lunch break is staggered and people take it in turns to eat while others continue working.

In other parts of the world, all the shops, schools, offices, and factories close in the middle of the day. The midday meal is an important one and people like to take their time over it. These tend to be the very hot countries where it is very difficult to work in the middle of the day when the sun is at its hottest. People have a long lunch and then take a rest—a siesta—after it. They go back to work later in the afternoon when it is not quite so hot.

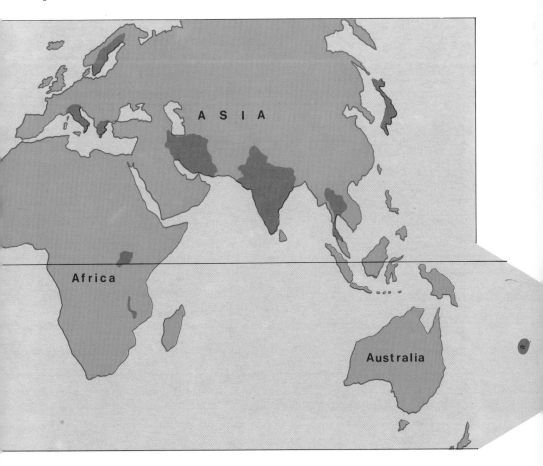

Sweden

In the past, the main meal for most Swedish families was at noon, but today with most parents at work all day, the main meal tends to be in the evening.

For many Swedes lunch is a light meal of one hot dish and a glass of milk. A cup of coffee finishes the meal. All Swedish schoolchildren get a free dinner, and many offices have their own cafeteria where the workers can buy a meal. Popular lunchtime dishes include fried herring, pea soup with pork, meatballs and *kalop*, which is a beef stew. Herring are a basic food in Swedish cookery. People enjoy eating them smoked, pickled, and marinated.

Left *A Laplander cuts reindeer meat for cooking over an open fire.*

Above *A tempting array of open sandwiches.*

The Swedes are also famous for smorgas, which are open sandwiches. An open sandwich is a slice of bread and butter topped with a slice of cheese, sausage, fish, egg, or ham and salad. This is not covered with another slice of bread like our sandwiches; instead it is left 'open.' The bread used for smorgas is made with molasses and is quite moist. Smorgas can be eaten at any time though many people do eat them as a quick lunchtime meal.

Italy

Because the summers are very hot in Italy, all the offices, schools, and shops close in the middle of the day so that everyone can go home to eat. The Italians like to eat a large meal with many, varied courses.

They may begin the meal with *antipasta*, which could be shellfish or melon, but most families start with a pasta course. There are many different types of pasta—one that you have probably eaten is spaghetti. Pasta is made from eggs, flour, and oil. Some people make their own, but it is often more convenient to buy it ready-made, either fresh or dried, from stores.

Pasta comes in every shape you can think of. There are strips of pasta called tagliatelli and very broad bands called lasagna. It is also pressed into shell shapes, twisted into spirals, or made into letters of the alphabet. It can be filled

Left *Making ravioli — pasta parcels filled with meat.*

Right *Diners at a restaurant share a bottle of wine over the* antipasta *course.*

with meat—called ravioli, or long rolls called cannelloni. Otherwise, the cooked pasta is eaten with a sauce.

The next course will usually be either veal, beef, chicken, or fish with salad. Each region will have its own special way of cooking these dishes. The Italians always like to eat fresh bread with their meal. To finish there is fruit, cheese, or ice cream, and coffee served very strong in tiny cups.

Greece

Lunch is served at around 2 P.M. and lasts for about an hour. It will begin with simple appetizers called *mezze*—perhaps little squares of *feta* (goat's milk cheese), sliced tomatoes, peppers and olives; or maybe a rich fish-roe pâté called *taramasalata*, *dolmades* (stuffed vine leaves), or *keftethakia* (tiny, spicy meatballs). The main course will probably be seafood—fish, lobster, squid, and shellfish are all very popular—accompanied by a vegetable or salad dish and bread. A well-known Greek salad is made of onions, tomatoes, cucumbers, olives, and a dressing. Perhaps you have tried another famous Greek dish—*moussaka*, which is made from eggplant, ground meat, white sauce, and cheese.

Left *Octopus hanging up to dry by a taverna.*

Above *Enjoying a lobster lunch in a beautiful coastal setting.*

After the meal there is fruit such as apricots, peaches, melons, grapes, and figs, which all grow well in Greece's hot climate. This climate allows families to eat their meals out in the open for much of the year.

For hundreds of years Greece was occupied by invaders from other countries, who brought their own ideas to Greek cookery. Modern Greek food has many Italian and Turkish-style dishes—pasta, kebabs, rich sweet pastries, and strong dark coffee.

AFRICA
Malawi

Most African countries, including Malawi, do not have such a good diet as we do and many of the poorer people become ill from a lack of protein and other nutriments. The staple food of the Malawians is maize (corn), which is partially pounded, soaked, and then ground. This removes all protein and vitamins—unfortunately—leaving pure white cornstarch. This is used to make porridge (which is harder than the sort we might eat) called *nsima* which is eaten with vegetables to make the meal. These vegetables might be cabbage, chopped pumpkin leaves, or any others available at the time, perhaps served with *nkhuani* relish. Some of the vegetables are often mixed up with groundnut (peanut) flour, tomatoes, and onions. Beans, peas, pulses (seeds), groundnuts, sweet potatoes, and

Right *Smoking fish—this preserves them so that they can be kept longer without going bad.*

Left *Sugarcane sellers in a market. Children like to suck pieces of cane like a lollipop.*

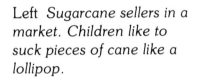

cassava roots are all commonly eaten. Some people eat rice, often with milk and vegetables.

Meat is eaten on special occasions, and fish sometimes —when people can afford it. In some areas, chicken, eggs, and fish are believed to make women unable to have babies, so women are not allowed to eat those foods.

Fruit may finish the meal—bananas, mangoes, pineapples, pawpaws, or perhaps fried guavas. Children like pieces of sugarcane, which they suck like a lollipop.

29

Uganda

The main part of the midday meal in Uganda is made from a local staple food—either plantains, sweet potatoes, cassava, millet, sorghum, maize, or yams. To go with this there are side dishes made from beans, peas, and groundnuts, and perhaps eggs, meat, or fish. Some of the side dishes are more like soups, and these may be served in bowls made from gourds, called calabashes.

One main dish is a porridge called *matoke* made from plantains, which are a kind of green banana. First of all the women cut some fruit and leaves. An iron or aluminum pot is used to cook the matoke. The pot is lined with leaves, then enough water to cover the lining is poured in, the bundle of plantains is laid inside, and finally more leaves are added to make a lid.

Cooking is done outside in the dry season, but in the rainy season the women use a small kitchen which is separate from

Left *Shopping for plantains in a busy banana market.*

Right *Cooking* matoke *in big metal pots.*

the house. The pot stands on large stones and a fire is lit beneath it. The contents are cooked for about an hour and a half, then the bundle of plantains is taken out and pressed in a basket to make a soft paste. This goes back into the pot for at least another hour's cooking. The finished matoke is a golden yellow color.

Most people eat with their fingers, so hands must be washed before the meal. A portion of the main dish is scooped up, and dipped into one of the side dishes before it is put in the mouth.

Above A boy uses a
specially-adapted bicycle to
deliver a batch of flat bread
called Non.

Right Cooking kebabs in
Tehran.

Iran

Rice is the daily staple food for many people in Iran. In the area around the Caspian Sea, the provinces of Gilan and Mazandaran, and on the slopes of the Alborz Mountains, farmers grow fields of rice. Iranians have two basic methods of serving rice—either as *chelo* or as *polo*. Chelo is steamed rice that is served with different meats and sauces. Polo, which we often call 'pilaf' or 'pilau,' is rice with other ingredients mixed into it.

The main meats eaten in Iran are lamb and chicken. These can both be used to make *shish kebabs*—cubes of meat and vegetables pushed onto a skewer and grilled over a hot fire. Another popular way of serving meat is a *khoresh*, a thick sauce or stew with vegetables, fruit, nuts, herbs, and spices. These dishes, which are often hot and spicy, are always served with rice. Yogurt, which is an important ingredient in Iranian cookery, is served with the meat course.

India

There are several different cooking styles in India, which come from the traditional upper middle class (Brahmin or top caste) cookery in a particular area. But there may be enormous variations according to religion, caste, and how wealthy a family is.

We will look at a typical meal for a family in a village in northwest India, where wheat is the main food. Here people can only afford to eat twice a day—at about 10 A.M. and 6 P.M. They will eat more or less the same meal at both times. Wheat is used to make *dhullia* (porridge) and *chapatties* (bread). These are served with such vegetables as onions, beans, eggplant, pumpkins, and squash-like vegetables, which are curried by seasoning with various spices such as chilies, garlic, and root ginger. Lentils are also eaten.

Right *Cooking* chapatties
on a communal stove.

Left *Villagers drying grain*
under the hot sun.

At mealtime, everyone sits cross-legged on the ground. Each person is given dhullia or chapatties, a bowl of lentils, and some vegetable curry. People break off a piece of chappati and scoop up the curry with it. Sometimes there is not enough of these foods and the family must go hungry. An orange, a few peanuts, or rice would be special treats.

In this area the people are orthodox Hindus and believe it is wrong to kill animals. They do not eat meat, fish, or eggs, and so their diet is lacking in important body-building protein. What about milk? Even if a family has a cow or goats, the animals have so little to eat that they hardly give any milk. The milk is usually sold anyway to provide money for essential goods like clothes and cooking oil.

There is no tea or coffee to drink, either. These crops are not grown in this part of India and are too expensive to buy. Water is the only drink.

35

Thailand

When you are asked to a meal in Thailand, the words used actually mean 'come and eat rice.' Indeed, all Thai dishes are eaten with rice—which grows there very easily as the climate is very warm and there is lots of rain.

The food is always served in neatly cut up pieces, so there is no need to use knives and forks; instead, special spoons and forks are used. The Thais used to eat with their hands and there are still some people who eat this way. There is a particular way of doing it. First they wash their right hand in a bowl of water—they only eat with this hand. They are careful not to let the food touch the palm of their hand. After the meal the hand is again carefully washed.

The meal is made up of many different dishes, all of which are spicy. These dishes or soups are served in bowls which everyone shares, though each person has his own bowl of rice. Each different dish is tasted on its own. The average meal in a well-to-do household will consist of at least four or five dishes, two or three sauces and soup, followed by desserts and several different fruits. Thailand is bordered by a long stretch of coast, and fish and shellfish are a very important part of Thai cooking. Pork and chicken are also popular.

Left *Grinding sweet corn to make gruel.*

Right *Traders sell their wares from boats at the floating market in Bangkok.*

Japan

The Japanese eat their midday meal at about noon. The meal, as in many other Asian countries, usually has rice in it, because rice grows there very easily and is a filling food. Asians eat rice in much the same way as we eat potatoes. The Japanese, however, do sometimes eat noodles instead of rice. Japan is an island country and so fish is readily available—and very popular. It is a major ingredient in Japanese cooking. Until recently the Japanese ate almost no meat at all because it was not thought to be in keeping with the teaching of their Buddhist religion, but today they do have some chicken, beef, and pork.

Besides white fish and shellfish, people also eat octopus, cuttlefish, shark, and globefish. Some famous local dishes are *sashimi*, thin slices of raw fish like carp, tuna, shark, whale, or lobster; *tempura*, small pieces of vegetables and fish quickly fried together in batter; and *sukiyaki*, beef and vegetables

Left *A family enjoys its midday meal together.*

Above *Two girls spend their lunch break in a Tokyo park.*

fried together like a fondue. The dishes are all served in bowls. Special porcelain ones are used for rice and laquered ones for soup. Tea is taken with the meal and this, too, is drunk out of bowls.

When eating their food, the Japanese use *hashi* (chopsticks), which are usually made of wood so they are cheap enough to be thrown away after use. They can also be made from ivory, bone, bamboo, or metal. There is one kind for eating, another for cooking, and a third for picking up cakes and other desserts.

Samoa

In the islands of Samoa, the midday meal is the main one of the day. Samoans are excellent fishermen, so seafood is often on the menu—shrimps, turtles, clams, sea urchins, tuna, mullet, and shark. Fish is wrapped in banana leaves and then baked. Pork and chicken are favorite meats. Taro (a root vegetable) and yams are eaten at every meal; breadfruit and cassava are also common. Breadfruit and young taro leaves are often baked in coconut cream.

The Samoans have a separate building called a *falekula* in which to cook their meals. It is built a few meters from the house and is made of wood, with slatted walls and a thatched roof. You have to stoop to enter but you can stand upright once you are inside. A cooking pot rests between two posts lying on the ground; underneath it there is a space to light a fire. To make an oven, a pit is dug in the ground and a fire is lit in it. Stones are put in to heat, and when they are hot enough, the fire is put out. Little parcels of food are placed on the hot stones, covered with banana leaves, and left to bake.

To eat their meal, the family sits cross-legged on the ground and the food is served on specially-woven mats.

Left *A breadfruit tree.*

Right *Fishing for seafood — the wide variety of these form the basis of many Samoan dishes.*

Mexico

Mexico is a tropical country, which means that it has a very hot, dry climate, and a rainy season. In the middle of the day it gets too hot to work, and all the shops and offices close. Mexicans eat their midday meal late, usually between two o'clock and half past five in the afternoon. This is the main meal of the day.

Each of Mexico's regions has a different style of cooking and uses food found readily in that area. From the coast come fish recipes; from the north, which is a great cattle-raising area, come beef recipes. Pigs are kept all over the nation, and pork is a common dish. Chicken, too, is very popular. Three food plants flourish in Mexico—maize (corn), beans, and squash—so much use is made of these in cooking. Mexicans like very hot, spicy food. Chilies, which are very hot-tasting peppers, are

Left *Father lets the baby try a taste of his meal.*

Above *Cooking tortillas in a street market.*

used to make these highly-seasoned dishes.

The meal is made up of many courses. These are soups and dishes of fish or vegetables. The main course is fish, meat, or poultry served with vegetables or salad. One famous Mexican dish which you may have had at home is *chili con carne*. It is a hot, spicy mix of meat, onions, beans, and chilies. The meal is often finished with a sweet pastry and a cup of thick black coffee.

Tortillas are a basic part of Mexican cookery, and are served with all meals. A tortilla is a flat round bread, rather like a thick pancake, made of maize. Poorer Mexicans use tortillas as a plate, and to wipe their mouths after eating! Tortillas are often filled with different things and rolled up. *Enchiladas* are tortillas filled with highly-seasoned beans, served with chili sauce. A *taco* is a tortilla which is filled and then fried.

Bolivia

Bolivia is very high up in a range of mountains called the Andes. Cooking methods here are different from those in other South American nations. At such high altitudes water boils at a lower temperature and so it takes longer to cook food—six minutes to boil an egg instead of three!

Potatoes are the main food in Bolivia. Bolivians preserve their potatoes by shredding them, then leaving them out to freeze at night and dry in the sunlight by day. After a few days the potatoes can be stored and kept for many months.

Bolivia has fine lake and river fish, such as *surubi* and *dorado*, as well as trout and smelt. Food is highly seasoned. *Locoto*, a type of chili pepper, is widely used in meat and vegetable dishes to make them hot and to add flavor.

Right *Potatoes form a large part of the Bolivian diet.*

Left *The market at Tihuanaca.*

A typical Indian meal will begin with chicken soup containing large pieces of chicken and flavored with herbs. This is followed by slices of roasted kid (young goat) and vegetables covered with a sauce. For dessert there is baked plantain or fresh fruit such as pawpaw.

Often though, people will eat one-dish meals, which must be warm and satisfying to keep out the cold. These may be *chupes*, a type of stew containing meats and poultry cooked with a variety of root and green vegetables.

Colombia

The midday meal is usually eaten between 12:30 P.M. and 1:30 P.M. For most people it is a big meal which will start with a soup. The main dish varies according to the area. In the east, people might enjoy roasted meat like chicken, beef, or veal with lots of beans or yucca (a root vegetable) and potatoes or rice. People who live along the coast make use of the fish that is readily available. Here, seafood is often cooked in coconut milk and served with dishes like rice with fried coconut and raisins. Specialities in the highland areas are potatoes with cheese sauce and stuffed flank steaks. Colombian food is subtly seasoned, and although there will be hot chili sauce on the table, people do not cover their food with large amounts of it.

Below Preparing maize for grinding.

Right Home-grown fresh fruit often finishes a meal.

One speciality of the country is *arepas*, which are corn buns made from a special flour ground from large-kernel white corn. These are delicious with fresh cream cheese. There are many types of arepas—some may be delicately flavored with cinnamon and then fried.

For dessert there is home-grown fruit, with oranges, coconuts, bananas, guavas, melons, pineapples, and many others to choose from. Black coffee is served after the meal.

Recipes

BAKED CORN
from Bolivia

Ingredients:
311g (11oz) canned sweet
  corn or 5 ears fresh corn
2 eggs
14g (½oz) margarine
⅛ level teaspoon chili
  powder
1 clove garlic or level
  teaspoon aniseed
1 level teaspoon flour
100g (4oz) swiss or goat's
  milk cheese (cheddar will
  do if you cannot get this)

Equipment:
large casserole dish
frying pan
2 small bowls

1. Scrape kernels from uncooked corn, or open can of corn
   if using this.
2. Beat eggs and combine with corn.
3. Heat fat, add chili powder, aniseed, or garlic and flour
   and cook for one minute in frying pan.
4. Mix into corn and eggs.
5. Pour half of the mixture into a well-greased 0.85 liter
   (1½ pint) casserole and cover with thin slices of cheese.
   Pour remaining corn mixture on top.
6. Cover and cook for forty-five minutes in a moderate oven
   (350°F/180°C). Serves three to four.

KEBABS
from Iran

Ingredients:
6 cubes of lamb
3 sheep's kidneys
6 small mushrooms
6 small tomatoes
oil for frying
12 bay leaves

Equipment:
bowl
small knife
6 skewers
brush

1. Skin the kidneys and take out core. Cut in half and soak in cold water for five minutes.
2. Peel mushrooms, then brush all ingredients with oil.
3. Thread meat, kidneys, mushrooms, and tomatoes alternately onto the skewers with a bay leaf at each end.
4. Grill for ten to fifteen minutes.

FETTUCINE ALLA POMODORO
(Ribbon pasta with fresh tomato sauce)
from Italy

Ingredients:
1 package of fettucine
3 cloves of garlic
6 ripe tomatoes
olive oil
herbs—basil, parsley, mint
salt and pepper
grated cheese

Equipment:
large saucepan
small saucepan
wooden spoon
sharp knife

1. Boil water in the large pan for the pasta, put it in to cook (see instructions on the package).
2. Put some oil into the smaller saucepan, slice the garlic, and cook it in the hot oil.
3. Cut up the tomatoes and add them to the oil as well. Cook for about three minutes, then put in basil, mint, or parsley.
4. Season with salt and pepper.
5. When the fettucine has cooked, drain it and pour this sauce over it. Serve in bowls with grated cheese on top.

This sauce is good with all kinds of pasta and rice.

CURRIED FISH CUTLETS
from Thailand

Ingredients:
3 whiting
9 dried chilies
1 slice of ginger
1 onion
7 cloves of garlic
½ teaspoon shrimp paste
1 egg
oil
½ lemon

Equipment:
pestle and mortar
sharp knife
frying pan
chopping board
spoon for mixing

1. Squeeze the lemon into the bowl and then add chilies, ginger, shrimp paste, garlic, and onion and grind it into a paste with the pestle.
2. Clean the whiting and fillet it.
3. Coat the fish fillets in the paste. Beat the egg and dip the fillets in it.
4. Remove the fish covered in the paste and egg and fry in deep oil until brown.
5. Serve with rice.

VEGETABLE SALAD
from Colombia

Ingredients:
3 Spanish-style sausages, diced (garlic sausages will do)
½ cup cooked green (runner) beans
½ cup sweet corn
½ cup lima or kidney beans
2 tomatoes, peeled and diced
1 small head lettuce
⅓ cup olive oil
⅓ cup vinegar
3 spring onions, chopped
1 tablespoon minced parsley
1 clove garlic, crushed
1 teaspoon salt
¼ teaspoon pepper

1. In a large bowl, mix the sausage with the vegetables and lettuce (torn into small pieces).
2. Mix the rest of the ingredients and pour over the salad.
3. Toss, chill and serve.

CHAPATTIES
from India

Ingredients:
225g (8oz) whole wheat
   flour
pinch salt
150ml (¼ pint) plus
   2 tablespoons water
melted butter

Equipment:
pastry board
rolling pin
heavy frying pan

1. Sieve flour and salt onto a pastry board or a large plate.
2. Make a hole in a center of the flour and add eight tablespoons of the water. Knead well for fifteen minutes to form a soft dough.
3. Add the rest of the water gradually, kneading for another ten minutes.
4. Let it stand for thirty minutes.
5. Divide into ten to twelve portions and roll out into thin round pancakes.
6. Meanwhile heat a griddle or heavy frying pan, then cook one chappati at a time. Do not use any oil. Press to flatten when small blisters appear on the surface, then turn and cook on the other side until the chapatti is lightly golden.
7. Brush a little butter on one side and serve.

KARRIDAKIA
sweets from Greece

Ingredients:
225g (8oz) dried figs
225g (8oz) pitted dates
100g (4oz) shelled walnuts
50g (2oz) sugar
1 teaspoon cinnamon

Equipment:
chopping board
large bowl
small bowl

1. Chop figs, dates, and walnuts, or mince them.
2. In the large bowl, mix them thoroughly together and roll into balls about an inch in diameter.
3. Mix sugar and cinnamon together in small bowl. Roll balls in this mixture until well coated. Makes about 30 sweets.

3 · Food for life: Eating rules our lives

As we all need to eat regularly, we have to set aside enough time to buy, prepare, cook, and eat our food. The main meal of the day may traditionally be either at midday or in the evening, depending on where you come from; but no matter which country you live in, you will still have to arrange your life to allow time for it. Whether you are at work or at school, there is time set aside for eating in the middle of the day.

Large stores make their clerks stagger their lunch breaks so that the stores do not have to close in the middle of the day. Many of their customers will want to do their shopping in their own lunch hour, so the stores must arrange to have more clerks serving at this busy time.

Eating affects our family life, too. Most families like to eat at least one meal a day at which they can all be together—how does your family arrange this? But our eating patterns are changing. We buy more convenience foods, which make it possible for individual members of the family to cook and eat by themselves. Most mothers go out to work and do not want to spend a long time cooking when they get home. Television has encouraged us to eat food that is quick to prepare and eat, so that we do not miss a favorite program. We may not even sit round a table together, eating our meal instead from trays while watching television.

A day spent on the beach means planning what food to take with us. This family is eating paella on a Majorcan beach.

What people will not eat

There is no food that people cannot eat, but there are some foods that people will not eat, for different reasons. Even very hungry people will not eat certain foods. Food taboos are often due to religious beliefs. In India, many people follow the Hindu religion. To them, the cow is considered to be a sacred animal, so it is not killed for food. Hindus believe that after we die, we can be born again as a different person, or even as an animal. So, very strict Hindus are vegetarians—they never eat meat—because they do not want to risk eating another person.

Jews have very strict rules about what they may or may not eat—pork is forbidden, and so is rabbit and some seafood. Animals must be killed in a certain way so that the blood drains out of the body. Meat may not be eaten in the same meal as anything containing milk, and separate dishes and pans are used to cook meat and dairy dishes.

Vegetarians are a group of people who do not believe that we should kill animals for our food and will not eat meat of any sort. Their diet is made up of beans, cheese, nuts, pasta, and different vegetables. Some vegetarians carry this idea further and will not eat products which we get from animals—like milk, cheese, butter, and eggs.

In our society, unlike some in Asia, there are certain animals that we do not like to have killed for meat—such as cats, dogs, or hamsters. We think of them as pets and not food animals.

Right *Vegetarians must get their protein from foods like these.*

Left *Jewish people have strict rules about what they eat. Here a rabbi checks* matzot *(unleavened bread) for Passover.*

Cooking our food

Food is cooked to make it more digestible, to kill germs and make it safe, and to make it more pleasant to eat. Making food more digestible means that it can be more easily used by our body once it has been swallowed. Many foods cannot be digested until they have undergone a chemical or mechanical change in the cooking process. Carbohydrates are changed by heat into a form that is easier for us to digest. This is a chemical change. The cellulose membranes in vegetables are broken down by cooking—this is a mechanical change. Meat is made more tender by cooking, so it is easier to chew!

Sometimes, if we do not take care, we lose some of the nourishment in food by overcooking it. If some vegetables are boiled for too long, the vitamin C they contain is destroyed. Vitamin B, too, is destroyed by high temperatures.

Below *Spit-roasting a pig over an open fire.*

Right *A chef has to learn many different ways of cooking food.*

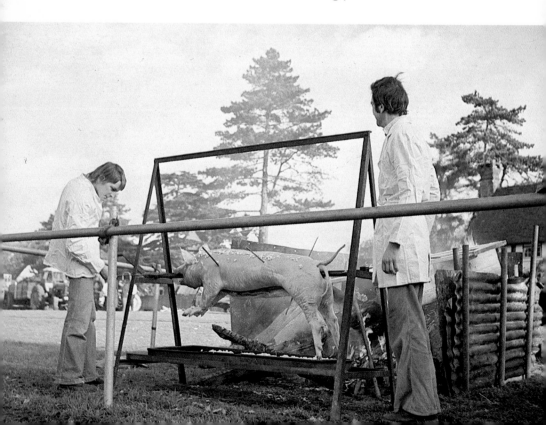

Although people eat food in many different ways around the world, there are only a few basic methods of cooking it. We can *boil* or *stew* food by cooking it in a pan with some liquid. We can *bake* or *roast* by putting the food in an enclosed box full of very hot air—an oven! We can *fry* food by putting it in a pan of hot fat or oil. Or food can be *grilled* or *broiled* by placing it underneath heat.

Other methods are spit-roasting over a fire and cooking in steam. One way of using steam is in a pressure cooker—this is a very strong enclosed pan which cooks the food quickly by the pressure of the steam which builds up inside the pan. The most modern way of cooking is the microwave oven, which can cook food in minutes rather than hours.

What happens when we eat?

What happens when you put food in your mouth? You chew it up—sharp front teeth bite into it and back teeth grind it small enough to swallow. Saliva mixes in with it, then you swallow. The ball of food is pushed down a tube called the esophagus by various muscles and into your stomach.

The food stays in your stomach while digestive juices break it down into a liquid. The liquid food is then passed into the duodenum, where it is broken down further, and next into the intestines. Tiny blood vessels in the walls of the intestines absorb the nutriments from the food into the bloodstream.

The blood carries the nutriments to the liver where a chemical reaction changes them so that they can be used by the body. Blood carries the nutriments to all parts of the body. Some help our muscles to move and some rebuild the worn parts such as our skin. The unused food that is left in the intestines is waste and is not needed to help the body in any of its tasks. These waste products, called feces, are passed out of the body through the rectum and anus.

The body's digestive system. This is the route that food takes after you swallow it, to get to the stomach. From here the food moves into the intestines where some of it is converted into nutriments to be used by the body, while the waste products are passed to the rectum to be excreted.

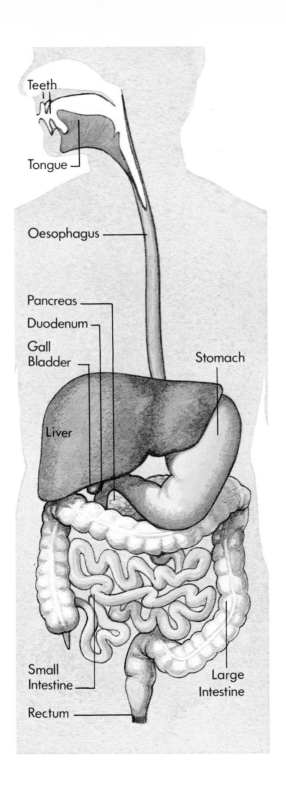

Teeth

Tongue

Oesophagus

Pancreas

Duodenum

Gall
Bladder

Stomach

Liver

Small
Intestine

Large
Intestine

Rectum

Glossary

ADDITIVES   Substances which manufacturers add to food to preserve it, and also to change its appearance, taste, and texture.

ANTIPASTA   Eaten by Italians before the main course—dishes like shellfish or melon.

CARBOHYDRATES   Potatoes, bread, cake, and cookies are all in this group of foods. Carbohydrates give us energy and keep us warm.

CASTE   The Hindu class system.

CHOPSTICKS   Small, thin sticks made of wood, bamboo, or bone. A pair of these is used by each person for eating in Japan and other Far Eastern countries.

DIGESTION   The process by which food is broken down in the stomach so that it can be used by the body.

EXPORT   To sell goods or produce to other countries.

GROUNDNUTS   Another name for peanuts.

KEBAB   Small pieces of meat and vegetables put on a skewer and grilled.

MALNUTRITION   A diet which is not properly balanced, or an insufficient diet, will result in malnutrition. This causes ill health and, if severe, death.

MARINATE   To soak meat or fish in a spiced liquid mixture before cooking.

MEZZE   Foods eaten as a first course in Greece.

NUTRIMENT   Any substance which provides nourishment for the body.

PASTA   Cooked dough made from eggs and flour in many different shapes and sizes. It comes from Italy.

PIZZA   A flat piece of bread covered with tomatoes, cheese, anchovies, mushrooms, and many other items. Pizzas come from Italy.

PROTEIN   Meat, fish, eggs, and nuts are all part of the protein group of foods. These are essential body-building foods.

SHELLFISH   Small creatures living in the sea, with a shell to protect them —like crabs, oysters, shrimps, or winkles.

SMORGAS   A piece of bread with a savory topping. Smorgas are eaten in Sweden.

SIESTA   An afternoon rest that is taken after the midday meal in many hot countries like Spain and Italy.

STAPLE FOOD   The main food of a country's people. If it lacks essential protein, vitamins, and minerals, it will cause the people who rely on it to become malnourished.

TORTILLAS   Flat bread made out of maize flour and eaten in Mexico.

VITAMINS AND MINERALS   Substances found in certain foods, which are essential to good health. We only need a small amount of them every day.

YOGURT   Fermented milk that has gone almost solid. It is often served as an accompaniment to spicy food in some countries.

Finding out more

The following organizations may be able to help with information on various foods, aspects of diet, or meals around the world.

American Institute of Nutrition, 9650 Rockville Pike,
Bethesda, MD 20814
4-H Clubs Extension Service, U.S. Department of Agriculture,
Washington D.C. 20250
Future Farmers of America, Box 15160, Alexandria, VA 22309
Future Homemakers of America, 2010 Massachusetts Ave. NW,
Washington D.C. 20036
National Association of Food Processors, 1133 20th Street NW,
Washington D.C. 20036
National Dairy Council, 6300 North River Road, Rosemont,
IL 60013
National Health Council, 70 W. 40th St., New York, New York
Public Health Association of America, 1015 15th Street NW,
Washington D.C.
U.S. Committee for World Health, 777 United Nations Plaza,
New York, NY 10017
World Health Organization, Avenue Appia 1211, Geneva 27,
Switzerland

Index

Picture acknowledgments

J. Allan Cash 25, 26, 29, 34, 44, 45; Elisabeth Photo Library 4 (below),
14, 42, 56; Richard and Sally Greenhill 9; Robert Harding Picture
Library 43; H. J. Heinz & Company 13; Alan Hutchison Library 28, 31,
35, 37, 46; Japan Information Centre 38; Mattessons Meats 12; John
Mitchell 20-21; Oxfam 36; Picturepoint 4 (above), 6, 8, 10, 15, 16, 17,
22, 27, 30, 32, 33, 39, 40, 54, 55, 57; South African Citrus Co-
operative 18; John Topham Picture Library 24, front cover; UNICEF
47; United States Travel Service 7, 11; Malcolm Walker 59.